K.D.'S JOURNEY

ISBN:978-1-958150-52-8
K.D.'s Journey

First publication: September 2025

Published by **Inner Peace Press**
Eau Claire, Wisconsin, USA
www.innerpeacepress.com

For my three C's.
For Pa, forever in our hearts.

Kira's Drawing, or K.D. for short, needed a little more pink, just a smidge more green. "There," Kira exclaimed. "She's perfect!"

K.D. felt pride and joy, blinking her eyes as she woke up.

"You'll be such a great surprise for Grandpa," K.D. heard Kira say.

While K.D. waited to meet Kira's grandpa, she got to know her own grandpa.

Party

He gave the best bear hugs and had the deepest barrel laughs.

He played tea-party for hours, sang the silliest songs, and tickled K.D. until she wheezed between giggles.

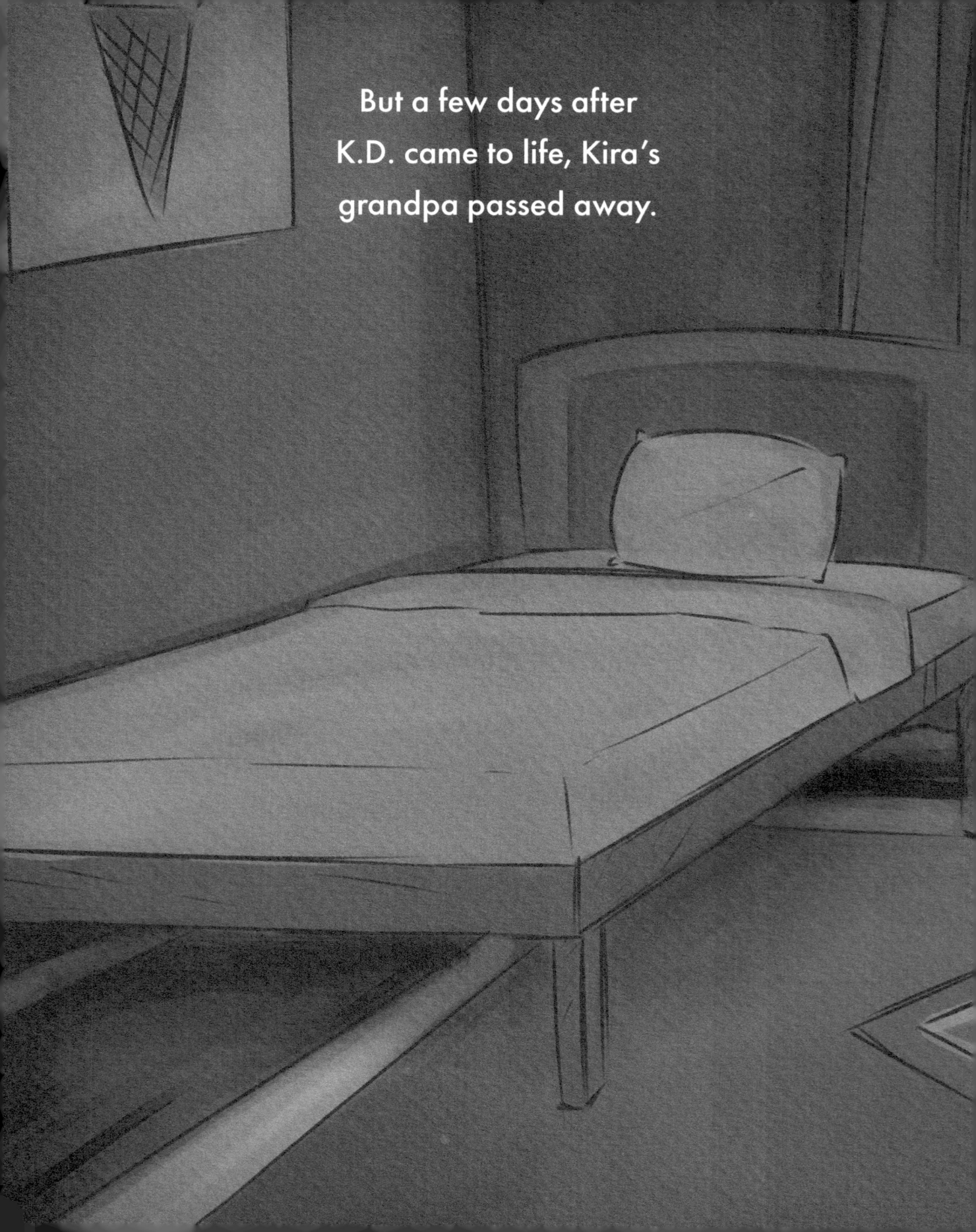

But a few days after K.D. came to life, Kira's grandpa passed away.

K.D.'s grandpa stopped hugging.

Stopped laughing.

Stopped playing.

As Kira rushed into her room and threw herself on her bed, K.D. was shoved under, into darkness.

"Oh no... What's going to happen to me now," she worried, feeling lost and scared.

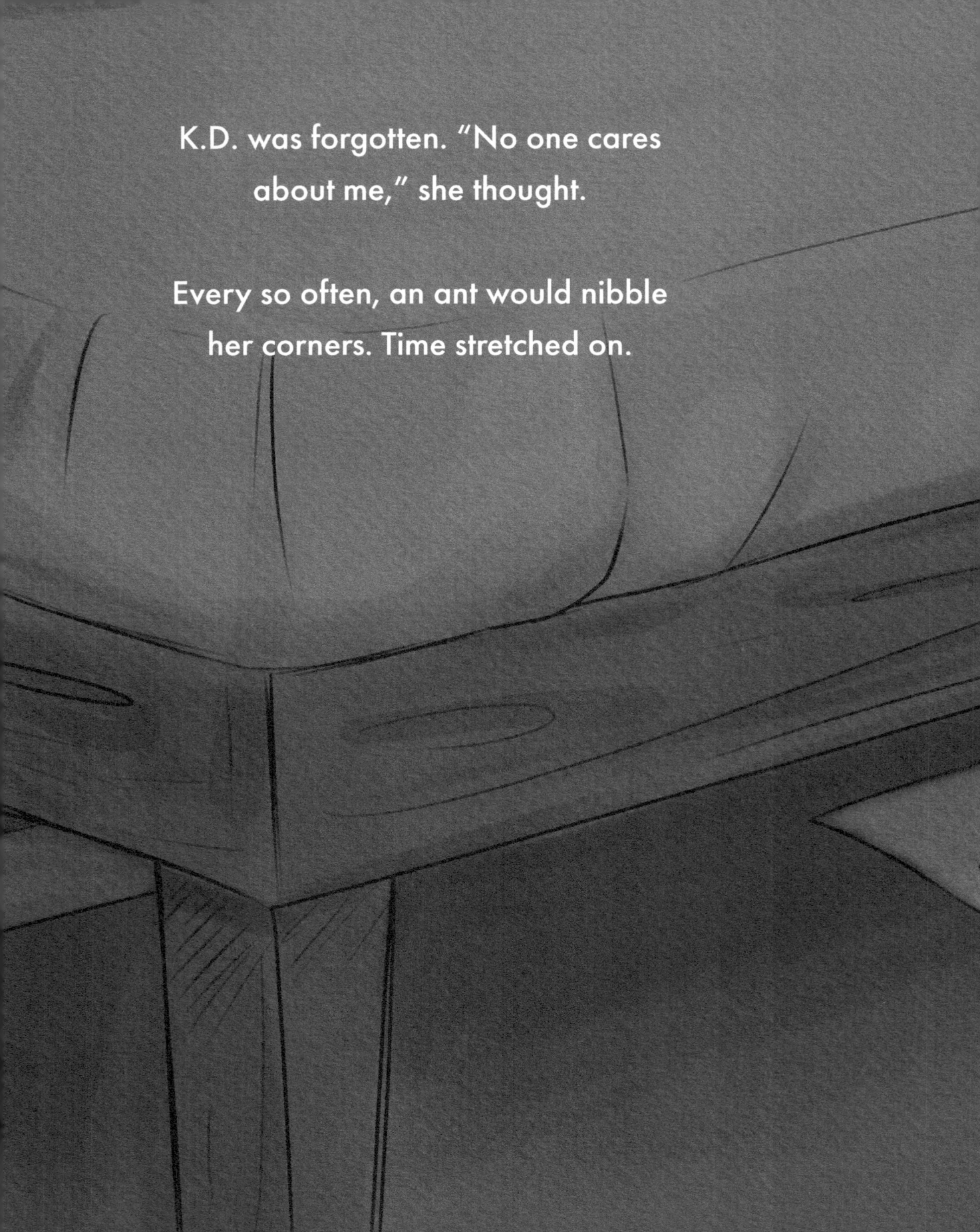

K.D. was forgotten. "No one cares
about me," she thought.

Every so often, an ant would nibble
her corners. Time stretched on.

One day, as Kira started to draw again, K.D. convinced the ants to drag her to the edge of the bed. "I'll tell you where some scrumptious crumbs are," she said.

Hope rose in K.D.'s heart as Kira gasped, "I've got to find a way to get my drawing to Grandpa!"

"I can't wait to meet Kira's grandpa," K.D. thought.

Being folded into a paper airplane was a bit uncomfortable.

Being thrown into the air was fun!

The fun ended as she glided to the ground.

"Harrumph," she thought
of her flight to nowhere.

"This should get me to the clouds," she hoped.

She rose higher than before, but still crashed to the ground.

K.D. buzzed with excitement. A promising launch
led to a thrilling trajectory towards the heavens.

Her heart sank as
fast as the rocket,
until it crashed into
the ground and
broke into pieces.

"It's no use," K.D. sighed, giving up on her dream of blasting off into space.

Frumpled and crumpled, K.D.
peered up through tears. "Huh...
that's really high," she thought.

"Oooof!" K.D. did not enjoy being shoved into Kira's pocket. After her stuffy ride home, K.D. listened to the muffled conversation.

"Dad! Dad! I saw this really big balloon going into the clouds at the park! Do you know what it was?"

"Oh, um, what did it look like?" Kira's dad asked.

K.D. nodded as Kira described the balloon. "It was really round, and white, and had something hanging from the bottom."

"That sounds like a weather balloon. It's used by meteorologists to study weather."

"Thanks, Dad! Gotta go!"

K.D. gratefully gulped air as she was pulled out from the stuffy pocket. It took her a while to fall asleep, even after such a tiring day.

The next morning, curiosity stopped K.D. midway through stretching.

"Uh huh... Okay... You mean I can come, too?" Kira asked. "Oh! Woohoo! Thank you so much for taking my drawing up on your next launch!" K.D. couldn't stop dancing!

A few days later, K.D. found herself clipped to the outside of an instrument box. She fluttered with nerves and excitement in the breeze.

"This has to work! It HAS to! I'm going to make it this time! I'm going to meet Kira's grandpa," K.D. thought.

Five, four, three, two, one.... LIFTOFF!

The warm air rustled K.D.'s edges, turning colder as she drifted higher. She grew nervous as the clouds grew larger and grayed. The air thinned and swirled faster.

"I never knew flying could be so fun! And look at how small everything is below," K.D. mused looking down. She began to worry when the clips started to freeze over and loosen. The balloon drifted higher still.

WHOOOOOSH!

"Agggghhhhh!" K.D. yelled as she was blown away!

"I'm lost again," K.D. cried as she fell through clouds, and cold, and dark gray wetness. Soaked, scared, starting to rip, a gentle wind of soft prayer broke through the gray and carried her up, up, up.

Up beyond the dark, wet clouds.
Up beyond the cold.
Into bright, sunny warmth.
Into the hands of Kira's grandpa.

As the drawing unfolded, K.D.'s grandpa embraced her once again.

Children and caregivers can honor the loss of a loved one by performing activities like those listed below. These activities also provide an opportunity and environment to openly discuss feelings and concerns about death and loss.

 Create a memorial display. Decorate a photo frame that will hold a cherished picture of your loved one.

 Create a scrapbook using stickers, crayons, markers, glue, construction paper, and other art supplies to honor the memories with your loved one.

 Write a story, song, book, or poem about your loved one.

 Write a letter to your loved one. Place it at your loved one's final resting place.

 Plant a tree, flower, or garden in memory of your loved one.

 Create a memorial video honoring the memories of your loved one using sections of previous recordings. Add music or a spoken message, like a poem.

 Turn a loved one's favorite shirt into a pillowcase by wrapping it around a pillow, tying the sleeves, and tucking in the bottom. Hug or snuggle it when missing them.

 Sew together your loved one's favorite clothing —shirts, sweaters, shorts, and more—to create a meaningful memorial blanket that offers comfort and preserves cherished memories.

 Honor your loved one by donating time or resources to a meaningful nonprofit or religious organization they valued.

Visit www.CatherineClarkFelts.com to download a copy of the photo frame drawing and journal sheet.

Children often find it difficult to express their feelings, especially when coping with grief and loss. To support a child during this time, use the following questions to gently start a conversation. It's helpful if the adult caregiver also shares their own responses—this not only models emotional expression but also introduces the child to the vocabulary they can use to describe their own feelings.

- What did your loved one enjoy most?

- What do you miss most about your loved one?

- How would you like to honor your loved one's memory?

- What activity can we do together?

- What was your best day with your loved one?

- What is the hardest part of loss?

- How does it make you feel?

- How did you spend time with your loved one?

I MISS YOU

PASTE

PHOTO

HERE

i love you _____

The one thing I miss most about you is:

_____

_____

_____

If we had one more day together we would:

_____

_____

_____

My favorite day together was when we:

_____

_____

_____

The thing that is the hardest without you here is:

_____

_____

_____

Something that makes me feel better when I have a hard day is:

_____

_____

_____

A time we laughed together is when:

_____

_____

_____

The best advice you ever gave me was:

_____

_____

_____

When I found out you were gone, I felt:

_____

_____

_____

We both loved:

_____

_____

_____

If I could say one more thing to you, it would be:

_____

_____

_____

About the Author

Catherine Clark Felts lives in Yorktown, Virginia, with her three mischievous cats, two amazing daughters, and one loving and supportive husband. An avid runner, she finds the best time to mull over a book concept is during an early morning jog. Formerly a technical support team Director and degreed Bioprocess Engineer, she felt the call to write and continue the legacy that her grandmother (Catherine Clark the 4th) and mother (Catherine Clark the 5th) passed down to her. She hopes to make a positive impact on children and families as they immerse themselves in her stories.

Visit www.CatherineClarkFelts.com to discover more books by the author.

www.ingramcontent.com/pod-product-compliance
Lightning Source LLC
Chambersburg PA
CBHW041155120626
46547CB00020B/3228